# 14
# Scriptural Principles for Daily Living Vol. 7

# 14
# Scriptural Principles for Daily Living Vol. 7

"Your words are a flashlight to light the path ahead of me and keep me from stumbling."
[Psalm 119:105 TLB]

Anthony Adefarakan

GLOEM, CANADA

# CONTENTS

| | |
|---|---|
| Dedication | 1 |
| Acknowledgement | 2 |
| Introduction | 4 |
| **Principle #1** Be Still | 7 |
| **Principle #2** Only Two Statements | 11 |
| **Principle #3** It will still Happen | 14 |
| **Principle #4** Stand Out | 17 |

CONTENTS

| | | |
|---|---|---|
| **Principle #5** | Say No to Chains | 20 |
| **Principle #6** | Mount Olympus Principle | 22 |
| **Principle #7** | Joseph's 20% | 24 |
| **Principle #8** | His Integrity – Your Assurance | 28 |
| **Principle #9** | What You Don't Know About Storms | 32 |
| **Principle #10** | Freedom From Mental Captivity | 37 |
| **Principle #11** | Freedom From Men's Condemnation | 41 |
| **Principle #12** | Freedom From Barrenness | 44 |
| **Principle #13** | Freedom From Conformity Syndrome | 47 |

## CONTENTS

**Principle #14** | Dealing with Satan's Constant Temptations — 50

| Conclusion — 55

| WHY YOU REALLY NEED JESUS! — 56

| PRAYER POINTS — 61

| BECOME A FINANCIAL PARTNER WITH JESUS — 62

| About the Author — 65

| — 68

# Dedication

I dedicate this book to God Almighty for His goodness and faithfulness in making His Word available to me. All glory to His Holy Name.

Also to everyone desirous of a closer walk with God, living out His precepts on a daily basis, I am in agreement with you all and I decree that grace for a closer walk with God is coming upon you in Jesus' Name.

# Acknowledgement

I sincerely acknowledge my Eternal Father, Who alone is the Source of all wisdom. He is the Author and Finisher of my faith and it is of His fullness that the contents of this book have been drawn.

Also, I want to profoundly appreciate my dear parents – Prince and Mrs. Timothy Adefarakan – for bringing me up in the way of the Lord and for instilling righteousness consciousness in me. The wonderful education foundation I was given, coupled with their constant encouragement has empowered me to reach heights that were once beyond my imagination.

My most special appreciation goes to my sweetheart, Abisolami; without her help and support, I would never have enjoyed the conducive atmosphere needed to publish this book. I appreciate your love, encouragement, and the support you give at all times. Thank you so much. I love you, my Baby!

And to all my mentors in Ministry, I appreciate you all. Your investments in my life are not in vain. May the Lord reward you all in Jesus' Name.

# Introduction

Life on earth has been described as a form of pilgrimage with eternity as man's final destination.

1 Peter 2:11 TLB says:
*"Dear brothers, you are only visitors here. Since your real home is in heaven, I beg you to keep away from the evil pleasures of this world; they are not for you, for they fight against your very souls."*

And Hebrews 11:13 also says:
*"These men of faith I have mentioned died without ever receiving all that God had promised them; but they saw it all awaiting them on ahead and were glad, for they agreed that this earth was not their real home but that they were just strangers visiting down here."*

In the course of this brief earthly sojourn, we

are bound to face certain situations capable of generating questions like *'what step do I take?' 'where do I settle?' 'who do I marry?' 'will I be rich or poor?' 'how do I finance my projects?' 'how do I take good care of my family?' 'how do I know God's will for my life?'* just to mention a few. Usually, we find it difficult to provide correct answers to these questions due to our weak mortal nature.

However, there is a manual for this pilgrimage, which is the Word of God. The One Who designed this journey for us has put in the manual all we need to navigate our way successfully and to eventually end up on the glorious side of eternity when the pilgrimage is over. Little wonder David prayed in Psalm 119:19 – *"I am a stranger in the earth; hide not thy commandment from me"*.

The principles presented in this Volume 7 are all Bible-based and will deliver results every time they are applied because the Word of God is forever settled in Heaven (Psalm 119:89).

I pray as you read on, God's grace to apply these principles will rest upon you in Jesus' Name.

**Anthony Adefarakan.**

## Principle #1

# Be Still

Mark 4: 35-39 KJV says *"And the same day, when the even was come, he saith unto them, Let us pass over unto the other side. And when they had sent away the multitude, they took him even as he was in the ship. And there were also with him other little ships. And there arose a great storm of wind, and the waves beat into the ship, so that it was now full. And he was in the hinder part of the ship, asleep on a pillow: and they awake him, and say unto him, Master, carest thou not that we perish? And he arose, and rebuked the wind, and said unto the sea, Peace, be still. And the wind ceased, and there was a great calm."*

When it comes to obtaining assistance from God concerning any issue of concern, only Him is permitted to be 'awake'. If you are asking Him for help and you are still fully 'awake', struggling and making anxious efforts at getting the problems solved, He will keep 'sleeping' (remaining inactive) until you are exhausted. But if you wake Him up like His disciples did when the storm was threatening their lives according to the text above, and you choose to be still while He works on your behalf, you will soon be sharing testimonies.

When the children of Israel came face-to-face with the Red Sea, the Lord told them through Moses to be still, and before they knew what was happening, the Red Sea had parted, and their enemies of 430 years were silenced.

Exodus 14:13-18 KJV: *'And Moses said unto the people, Fear ye not, stand still, and see the salvation of the LORD, which he will shew to you to day: for the Egyptians whom ye have seen to day, ye shall see them again no more for ever. The LORD shall fight for you, and ye shall hold your peace.*

*And the LORD said unto Moses, Wherefore*

*criest thou unto me? speak unto the children of Israel, that they go forward: But lift thou up thy rod, and stretch out thine hand over the sea, and divide it: and the children of Israel shall go on dry ground through the midst of the sea. And I, behold, I will harden the hearts of the Egyptians, and they shall follow them: and I will get me honour upon Pharaoh, and upon all his host, upon his chariots, and upon his horsemen. And the Egyptians shall know that I am the LORD, when I have gotten me honour upon Pharaoh, upon his chariots, and upon his horsemen.'*

Also, Adam had to be put to rest while God worked on his problem of loneliness. It was while he was asleep (inactive) that the Lord took out one of his ribs and formed a woman for him. Genesis 2:21-22 KJV: *'And the LORD God caused a deep sleep to fall upon Adam, and he slept: and he took one of his ribs, and closed up the flesh instead thereof; And the rib, which the LORD God had taken from man, made he a woman, and brought her unto the man.'*

Please stop hindering God by your anxious moves; to enjoy His Intervention, you will have to BE STILL AND KNOW THAT HE IS GOD – Psalm 46:10!

## Principle #2

# Only Two Statements

Matthew 25:31-46 NKJV says *""When the Son of Man comes in His glory, and all the holy angels with Him, then He will sit on the throne of His glory. All the nations will be gathered before Him, and He will separate them one from another, as a shepherd divides his sheep from the goats. And He will set the sheep on His right hand, but the goats on the left. Then the King will say to those on His right hand, 'Come, you blessed of My Father, inherit the kingdom prepared for you from the foundation of the world: for I was hungry and you gave Me food; I was thirsty and you gave Me drink; I was a stranger and you took Me in; I was naked and you clothed Me; I was sick and you visited Me; I was in prison and you came to Me.'*

*"Then the righteous will answer Him, saying, 'Lord, when did we see You hungry and feed You, or thirsty and give You drink? When did we see You a stranger and take You in, or naked and clothe You? Or when did we see You sick, or in prison, and come to You?' And the King will answer and say to them, 'Assuredly, I say to you, inasmuch as you did it to one of the least of these My brethren, you did it to Me.'*

*"Then He will also say to those on the left hand, 'Depart from Me, you cursed, into the everlasting fire prepared for the devil and his angels: for I was hungry and you gave Me no food; I was thirsty and you gave Me no drink; I was a stranger and you did not take Me in, naked and you did not clothe Me, sick and in prison and you did not visit Me.'*

*"Then they also will answer Him, saying, 'Lord, when did we see You hungry or thirsty or a stranger or naked or sick or in prison, and did not minister to You?' Then He will answer them, saying, 'Assuredly, I say to you, inasmuch as you did not do it to one of the least of these, you did not do it to Me.' And these*

*will go away into everlasting punishment, but the righteous into eternal life.'"*

On the last day, when all is over; only two statements will proceed from the mouth of the Judge of the whole world - Jesus Christ. First, *'Weldone, thou good and faithful servant; enter into the joy of your Lord'*. Second, *'depart from me, you workers of iniquity into the lake of fire'*. Of course, no sane person will ever pray to hear that second statement. Everyone is hoping to hear the first one. Yes. But please take note of that first statement very well, He is going to say 'weldone', not well preached, well taught, well-spoken, well given, well studied, Church well attended BUT Weldone. God expects us to become DOERS OF HIS WORD AND NOT JUST HEARERS OR PREACHERS. So, if you will like to hear 'Weldone' on the last day, you will have to start doing whatever His Word says (Matthew 7:24-27, James 1:22-25).

## Principle #3

# It will still Happen

1 Thessalonians 4:13-17 NLT says *"And now, dear brothers and sisters, we want you to know what will happen to the believers who have died so you will not grieve like people who have no hope. For since we believe that Jesus died and was raised to life again, we also believe that when Jesus returns, God will bring back with him the believers who have died.*

*We tell you this directly from the Lord: We who are still living when the Lord returns will not meet him ahead of those who have died. For the Lord himself will come down from heaven with a commanding shout, with the voice of the archangel, and with the trumpet call of God. First, the believers who have died will rise from their graves. Then, together with them, we who are still alive and remain on the earth will be caught up in the clouds to meet the Lord in the air. Then we will be with the Lord forever."*

Just because your pastor is no longer preaching about the sudden uptake of the saints doesn't mean it will no longer happen. You need to forget about doctrinal arguments and focus on getting ready for the Master's return. Jesus is still coming again just as He promised in John 14:1-3 KJV: *'Let not your heart be troubled: ye believe in God, believe also in me. In my Father's house are many mansions: if it were not so, I would have told you. I go to prepare a place for you. And if I go and prepare a place for you, I will come again, and receive you unto myself; that where I am, there ye may be also.'*

We need to be ready at all times so that we don't miss it like the foolish virgins in the story the Lord told His disciples in Matthew 25:1-13 KJV: *'Then shall the kingdom of heaven be likened unto ten virgins, which took their lamps, and went forth to meet the bridegroom. And five of them were wise, and five were foolish. They that were foolish took their lamps, and took no oil with them: But the wise took oil in their vessels with their lamps. While the bridegroom tarried, they all slumbered and slept. And at midnight there was a cry made, Behold, the bridegroom cometh; go ye out to meet him. Then all those virgins arose, and trimmed their lamps. And the foolish said unto the wise, Give us of your oil; for our lamps are gone out. But the wise answered, saying, Not so; lest there be not enough for us and you: but go ye rather to them that sell, and buy for yourselves. And while they went to buy, the bridegroom came; and they that were ready went in with him to the marriage: and the door was shut. Afterward came also the other virgins, saying, Lord, Lord, open to us. But he answered and said, Verily I say unto you, I know you not. Watch therefore, for ye know neither the day nor the hour wherein the Son of man cometh.'*

My sincere prayer for you and your loved ones is that you will not miss your Heavenly flight in Jesus' Name. Stay alert!

## Principle #4

# Stand Out

2 Corinthians 6:14-18 KJV says *"Be ye not unequally yoked together with unbelievers: for what fellowship hath righteousness with unrighteousness? and what communion hath light with darkness? And what concord hath Christ with Belial? or what part hath he that believeth with an infidel? And what agreement hath the temple of God with idols? for ye are the temple of the living God; as God hath said, I will dwell in them, and walk in them; and I will be their God, and they shall be my people. Wherefore come out from among them, and be ye separate, saith the Lord, and touch not the unclean thing; and I will receive you, And will be a Father unto you, and ye shall be my sons and daughters, saith the Lord Almighty."*

Christians are Redeemed (Called-out) ones. The call to be a follower of Jesus Christ is a call to stand out. As a child of God, you can't afford to live a life that is in no way different from the way the heathen live. You are the light of the world; you are expected to be the standard others copy and not the other way round.

If you tell lies like every other person in your place of work, in what way are you different from them? If you cheat like everybody else, what makes you different? If all you do is love those who love you and hate those who don't, what makes you different from others? You can't stand out if you partake in the works of darkness as other people of the world.

Look at Isaiah 60:1-3 KJV: *'Arise, shine; for thy light is come, and the glory of the LORD is risen upon thee.*
*For, behold, the darkness shall cover the earth, and gross darkness the people: but the LORD shall arise upon thee, and his glory shall be seen upon thee.*

*And the Gentiles shall come to thy light, and kings to the brightness of thy rising.'*

You are the one the Lord has ordained to shine through the gross darkness that has covered the earth and the people living in it. You are called to rescue them through your light, and as such, you can't afford to live like the ones you have been called to rescue.

There is no relationship between light and darkness. To deliver people from the darkness that has covered them, you've got to let your light shine – and that means you have to stand out like a city that is set on a hill which cannot be hidden (Matthew 5:14).

Today, make a decision to always stand out.

## Principle #5

# Say No to Chains

Matthew 16:19 NLT *says "...I will give you the keys of the Kingdom of Heaven. Whatever you forbid on earth will be forbidden in heaven, and whatever you permit on earth will be permitted in heaven."*

Just to gently remind you that there is still power in the Name of Jesus Christ to break every chain - be it the chain of drug addiction, masturbation, smoking, flirting, telling lies, stealing, cheating, anxiety, indebtedness, mental disorder, loneliness, depression, suicide or whatever may be its nature. It is still standing as a chain because the Power in His Name is yet to be applied in faith.

In our opening text, Jesus Christ said whatever

you forbid on earth will be forbidden in heaven, and whatever you permit on earth will be permitted in heaven. That means your experiences on earth are based on what you permit or what you forbid. If you forbid sicknesses for instance, you are most likely going to live a healthy life; but if you do nothing about the sicknesses that attempt to colonize your body, you are simply permitting them to continue their operations in your body.

So, are there chains holding you down in certain areas of your life, preventing you from becoming what you feel the Lord has purposed for you to become? Go ahead and command those chains to break in the Name of Jesus and right there you will see them broken - John 14:14. And here is another good news, in case you are free from these chains you can also use the same power to break them in the lives of others. Hallelujah!

## Principle #6

# Mount Olympus Principle

Jeremiah 29:11 KJV says *"For I know the thoughts that I think toward you, saith the LORD, thoughts of peace, and not of evil, to give you an expected end."*

A particular student of a great philosopher once asked him, 'Sir, how can one get to Mount Olympus?' to which he answered, 'By making sure every step you take is towards Mount Olympus'.

Mount Olympus in this context is a goal you intend to achieve, a clearly defined destination that is especially time-bound. To achieve this, however, you've got to ensure every step you take, every relationship you choose, every money you make, every expenditure you incur, and every action you take are all geared towards getting to your 'Mount Olympus'.

If you live in Cameroon for instance, no matter how beautiful an airplane traveling to London may appear, if your intention is to travel to South Africa, it's not the right flight for you. To arrive in South Africa, you will have to take the flight scheduled for that location (even if it is unattractive), that's how you will get there.

Learn to apply this Mount Olympus Principle in your life and in your endeavours, especially every time you enter a New Year, and you will have a glorious ending. Remember that Jeremiah 29:11; the Lord only promises you an expected end. So, live and journey step by step towards your expectations, and before you know it, you will be there.

## Principle #7

# Joseph's 20%

Genesis 41:29-36 NLT says *"The next seven years will be a period of great prosperity throughout the land of Egypt. But afterward there will be seven years of famine so great that all the prosperity will be forgotten in Egypt. Famine will destroy the land. This famine will be so severe that even the memory of the good years will be erased. As for having two similar dreams, it means that these events have been decreed by God, and he will soon make them happen.*

*"Therefore, Pharaoh should find an intelligent and wise man and put him in charge of the entire land of Egypt. Then Pharaoh should appoint supervisors over the land and let them collect one-fifth of all the crops during the seven good years. Have them gather all the food produced in the good years that*

*are just ahead and bring it to Pharaoh's storehouses. Store it away, and guard it so there will be food in the cities. That way there will be enough to eat when the seven years of famine come to the land of Egypt. Otherwise this famine will destroy the land."*

Let us take some time and think about our finances. It is not unscriptural, neither is it unspiritual to critically analyze how money comes into our hands and how it goes out. Having to depend on paychecks to meet all our financial obligations is not a smart decision, and unfortunately that is exactly what we do. As of today, as soon as money comes into some people's hands, it quickly disappears because of one debt or the other that has to be settled.

However, there is good news. There is an opportunity to have a fresh start. Don't spend all your incomes meeting financial obligations, set some aside in order to acquire assets (ventures that can be putting money into your pocket aside your paycheck).

How did Joseph prepare for the time of lack according to our text? Firstly, he didn't wait for lack or the famine to set in before he started preparing. He prepared when there was still abundance. Secondly, he saved one-fifth (20%) of all the produce in the years of abundance towards making food available during the years of famine. Joseph saved just 20% and the entire nation of Egypt benefitted tremendously from it. They survived seven (7) years of national famine as a result.

On this planet, there are always seasons of abundance and seasons of lack. And the wisest thing you can do is to prepare for the season of lack during the season of abundance. That way, you will be able to escape the pain of lack when the season arrives.

Just by saving or investing 20% of your income, you can escape lack in the future. At least, Joseph proved it.

Don't just spend everything the Lord blesses you with; save and also become an investor!

# 14 SCRIPTURAL PRINCIPLES FOR DAILY LIVING
VOL. 7

## Principle #8

# His Integrity – Your Assurance

Isaiah 55:10-11 KJV says *"For as the rain cometh down, and the snow from heaven, and returneth not thither, but watereth the earth, and maketh it bring forth and bud, that it may give seed to the sower, and bread to the eater:*

*So shall my word be that goeth forth out of my mouth: it shall not return unto me void, but it shall accomplish that which I please, and it shall prosper in the thing whereto I sent it."*

When God says a thing, that thing must surely come to pass. God is a God of integrity and that's exactly why He is trustworthy.

Let's consider the integrity of Jesus' words. He said He would come back to life three days after His crucifixion and that's exactly what He did. Even while in the world of the dead, He kept to His word, how much more now that He is alive? That means you can bank on everything He says to you in His Word, none will fail.

It is also important to note that He rose from the dead very early in the morning. His resurrection wasn't delayed at all. Even in the world of the dead Jesus was time conscious. That means He will not delay in your case as well. He will come to your aid on time. You can actually trust Him.

Look at the promise God gave to Abraham and Sarah in Genesis 18:10-15 KJV: '*And he said, I will certainly return unto thee according to the time of life; and, lo, Sarah thy wife shall have a son. And Sarah heard it in the tent door, which was behind him. Now Abraham and Sarah were old and well stricken in age; and it ceased to be with Sarah after the manner of women. Therefore Sarah laughed within herself, saying, After I am waxed old shall I have pleasure, my lord being old also? And the LORD said unto Abraham, Wherefore did Sarah laugh, saying, Shall I of a surety bear a child, which am old? Is any thing too hard for the LORD? At the time appointed I will return unto thee, according to the time of life, and Sarah shall have a son. Then Sarah denied, saying, I laughed not; for she was afraid. And he said, Nay; but thou didst laugh.'*

That promise looked impossible, right? The conditions of Abraham and Sarah made that promise look like a joke that Sarah actually laughed.

But in Genesis 21:1-3 KJV, the integrity of God was proven in their lives: *'And the LORD visited Sarah as he had said, and the LORD did unto Sarah as he had spoken. For Sarah conceived, and bare Abraham a son in his old age, at the set time of which God had spoken to him. And Abraham called the name of his son that was born unto him, whom Sarah bare to him, Isaac.'*

That is the God we serve.

What has He promised you in a vision, through prophecies, or even in His Word? Believe, and expect Him to fulfill them regardless of how unlikely things may look. His integrity is your assurance of their fulfillment.

## Principle #9

# What You Don't Know About Storms

Mark 4:35-39 KJV says *"And the same day, when the even was come, he saith unto them, Let us pass over unto the other side. And when they had sent away the multitude, they took him even as he was in the ship. And there were also with him other little ships. And there arose a great storm of wind, and the waves beat into the ship, so that it was now full. And he was in the hinder part of the ship, asleep on a pillow: and they awake him, and say unto him, Master, carest thou not that we perish? And he arose, and rebuked the wind, and said unto the sea, Peace, be still. And the wind ceased, and there was a great calm."*

A close look at this text presents certain facts every believer in Christ should take note of.

Jesus Christ had just said to His disciples *"Let us cross over unto the other side"*. But between the time this statement was made and its actual fulfillment in Mark 5:1, something happened. The Bible says a great storm of wind arose and the waves beat into their ship. And from this we learn the following lessons:

- Storms of life usually come uninvited and without prior notice. You just never can tell when a storm will arise. Mark 4:37.

- Between where you are and where you want to be or are destined to be in life, you must encounter storms. That is, between the pronouncement and the fulfillment of your prophecies, storms must arise. Let us cross over to the other side (verse 35) was a prophecy – where they were going; but before they got there in Mark 5:1, there was a storm (chapter 4 verse 37).

- The Presence of God in your life will not prevent storms from arising in your life; however His Presence is your guarantee that you will overcome the storm. This means no level of spirituality will keep storms away; you are only assured of victory. Jesus was physically present in the ship, yet the storm arose (chapter 4 verses 35-39), John 2: 1-11, 2Kings 6:1-7.

- To benefit from His Presence however, you must "wake Him up" (chapter 4 verse 38). Even though He is in your boat, He won't intervene unless you consciously wake Him up or turn to Him for help. Until they woke Him up, He was still sleeping despite the great storm. Until they asked Him for help in John 2, He didn't turn their water to wine. James 4:2c says ye have not because ye ask not. Don't assume God will do something about your problem because He knows about it; He wants you to wake Him up through your prayers, worship, praises, sacrificial giving, meditating on His Word and reminding Him of what he has said concerning you in His Word.

- Note that he rebuked His disciples for their unbelief in verse 40; He expected them to have held on to His word which he told them before the journey began. He had told them "Let us cross over to the other side". The storm was a mere distraction but they saw it as *"carest not thou that we perish?"* When the Lord tells you anything, He expects you to believe it and consider it done regardless of the storm that may arise (Psalm 33:8-9). That is His expectation from us as believers. Focus on what He has said, the storm is a mere distraction. HIS WORDS MUST SURELY COME TO PASS, HE WILL NEVER LIE!

Say these prayers:
- I shield my life and family from every storm of life in the Name of Jesus.
- I crush every barrier to the fulfillment of my prophecies in Jesus' Name.
- Father, please let Your Presence continually abide with me and my family.
- Father, arise and turn my darkness to light.
- Father, don't let Your words fall to the ground over my life.

- Father, destroy every sign of unbelief in my heart. Please help my faith.
- I am victorious over every storm of life in the Name of Jesus.
Hallelujah!

## Principle #10

# Freedom From Mental Captivity

*Mark 5:1-20 KJV says "And they came over unto the other side of the sea, into the country of the Gadarenes. And when he was come out of the ship, immediately there met him out of the tombs a man with an unclean spirit, Who had his dwelling among the tombs; and no man could bind him, no, not with chains: Because that he had been often bound with fetters and chains, and the chains had been plucked asunder by him, and the fetters broken in pieces: neither could any man tame him. And always, night and day, he was in the mountains, and in the tombs, crying, and cutting himself with stones.*

*But when he saw Jesus afar off, he ran and worshipped him, And cried with a loud voice, and said, What have I to do with thee, Jesus, thou Son of the most high God? I adjure thee by God, that thou torment me not. For he said unto him, Come out of the man, thou unclean spirit. And he asked him, What is thy name? And he answered, saying, My name is Legion: for we are many. And he besought him much that he would not send them away out of the country. Now there was there nigh unto the mountains a great herd of swine feeding. And all the devils besought him, saying, Send us into the swine, that we may enter into them. And forthwith Jesus gave them leave. And the unclean spirits went out, and entered into the swine: and the herd ran violently down a steep place into the sea, (they were about two thousand;) and were choked in the sea.*

*And they that fed the swine fled, and told it in the city, and in the country. And they went out to see what it was that was done. And they come to Jesus, and see him that was possessed with the devil, and had the legion, sitting, and clothed, and in his right mind: and they were afraid. And they that saw it told them how it befell to him that was possessed with the devil, and also concerning the swine. And they began to pray him to depart out of their coasts. And when he was come into the ship, he that had been possessed with the devil prayed him that he might be with him. Howbeit Jesus suffered him not, but saith unto him, Go home to thy friends, and tell them how great things the Lord hath done for thee, and hath had compassion on thee. And he departed, and began to publish in Decapolis how great things Jesus had done for him: and all men did marvel."*

Mental challenges such as depression, anorexia, dementia, anxiety, hallucinations and even constant thoughts of suicide can at best be managed by medical professionals but never to be totally cured. To be totally free from these conditions, you need the Great Physician - His Name is Jesus. He takes such away free of charge without leaving any traces of them. Look at how He permanently cured the mentally challenged man in our text; the people who saw the man were simply amazed at his sudden transformation. Just tell Him you believe in Him and ask Him to set you free from your mental challenges. I guarantee you, they will all be gone for good.

Feel free to share your testimonies with us when this happens. Your freedom is here!

## Principle #11

# Freedom From Men's Condemnation

Romans 8:1-3 KJV says *"There is therefore now no condemnation to them which are in Christ Jesus, who walk not after the flesh, but after the Spirit. 2For the law of the Spirit of life in Christ Jesus hath made me free from the law of sin and death. 3For what the law could not do, in that it was weak through the flesh, God sending his own Son in the likeness of sinful flesh, and for sin, condemned sin in the flesh:"*

It is true that many of us commit sins, cover our weak points, break our promises and even nurture unholy thoughts during church services. But the Lord doesn't condemn us as men do. None of your sins is a surprise to Jesus, He knows about them all. And instead of making you feel bad, He is saying to you today *"I do not condemn you, go and sin no more"*. Guess what? You are now FREE!

He did that on one occasion when some people brought an adulterous woman to Him to have her condemned to death by stoning. Look at the story in John 8:3-11 KJV: *'And the scribes and Pharisees brought unto him a woman taken in adultery; and when they had set her in the midst, They say unto him, Master, this woman was taken in adultery, in the very act. Now Moses in the law commanded us, that such should be stoned: but what sayest thou? This they said, tempting him, that they might have to accuse him. But Jesus stooped down, and with his finger wrote on the ground, as though he heard them not.*

*So when they continued asking him, he lifted up himself, and said unto them, He that is without sin among you, let him first cast a stone at her. And again he stooped down, and wrote on the ground. And they which heard it, being convicted by their own conscience, went out one by one, beginning at the eldest, even unto the last: and Jesus was left alone, and the woman standing in the midst. When Jesus had lifted up himself, and saw none but the woman, he said unto her, Woman, where are those thine accusers? hath no man condemned thee? She said, No man, Lord. And Jesus said unto her, Neither do I condemn thee: go, and sin no more.'*

Why did He do that? It is because John 3:17 NKJV says *'For God did not send His Son into the world to condemn the world, but that the world through Him might be saved.'*

Are you experiencing men's condemnation? Talk to Jesus; He doesn't condemn. He only forgives and saves from sin (Matthew 1:21).

## Principle #12

# Freedom From Barrenness

Luke 1:5-14 KJV says *"There was in the days of Herod, the king of Judaea, a certain priest named Zacharias, of the course of Abia: and his wife was of the daughters of Aaron, and her name was Elisabeth. And they were both righteous before God, walking in all the commandments and ordinances of the Lord blameless. And they had no child, because that Elisabeth was barren, and they both were now well stricken in years.*

*And it came to pass, that while he executed the priest's office before God in the order of his course, According to the custom of the priest's office, his lot was to burn incense when he went into the temple of the Lord. And the whole multitude of the people were praying without at the time of incense. And there appeared unto him an angel of the Lord standing on the right side of the altar of incense. And when Zacharias saw him, he was troubled, and fear fell upon him. But the angel said unto him, Fear not, Zacharias: for thy prayer is heard; and thy wife Elisabeth shall bear thee a son, and thou shalt call his name John. And thou shalt have joy and gladness; and many shall rejoice at his birth."*

The first command God gave to man after creation was *"be fruitful..."* So, barrenness has no place in your life if you are connected to Jesus.

Zacharias and Elisabeth were both righteous before the Lord, yet they were childless. But because the Lord had commanded fruitfulness right from the time of creation, He visited them and made them joyful parents. Note however that despite their barrenness, Zacharias and his wife kept serving the Lord. And it was actually in the place of service that the Lord met them and solved their problem.

Are you believing God for a child or children of your own? Rejoice, your time has come. Put your hand on your belly and command your womb to carry babies in the Name of Jesus.

Keep serving the Lord, your visitation is very imminent.

## Principle #13

# Freedom From Conformity Syndrome

Romans 12:1-2 NKJV says *"I beseech you therefore, brethren, by the mercies of God, that you present your bodies a living sacrifice, holy, acceptable to God, which is your reasonable service. And do not be conformed to this world, but be transformed by the renewing of your mind, that you may prove what is that good and acceptable and perfect will of God."*

One of the greatest killers of destiny is the 'everybody-is-doing-it syndrome'. Customary thinking is the enemy of breakthrough thinking. You are a citizen of Heaven, and as such nothing should make you comprise your heavenly standards even when it hurts. From the experience of the three Hebrew men who were supernaturally delivered from the fiery furnace they were thrown into for refusing to bow down to the golden image set up by Nebuchadnezzar, and from the death of the soldiers who threw them in according to the Book of Daniel chapter 3, two laws were discovered:

First law - *'The Law of Faith'* which states that 'if you don't bow, you won't burn'.

And

Second law - *'The Law of Compromise'* which states that 'if you bow, you will burn'.

If you keep bowing down to what the world is bowing down to, you will keep experiencing the pains and sorrows the people of the world are experiencing. Just because everyone around you is consuming alcoholic drinks doesn't mean you should start drinking too. That's conformity. You should be able to say 'others may but I won't'. As a child of God, you are a divine brand and you shouldn't be living as the heathen. You are a spiritual eagle that is meant for the sky; you shouldn't be found flocking with chickens on the ground.

So, do you want to be free from the conformity syndrome? You need to be transformed by the renewing of your mind (through scriptural teachings and meditation).

## Principle #14

# Dealing with Satan's Constant Temptations

Matthew 4:1-11 KJV says *"Then was Jesus led up of the Spirit into the wilderness to be tempted of the devil. And when he had fasted forty days and forty nights, he was afterward an hungred. And when the tempter came to him, he said, If thou be the Son of God, command that these stones be made bread. But he answered and said, It is written, Man shall not live by bread alone, but by every word that proceedeth out of the mouth of God.*

*Then the devil taketh him up into the holy city, and setteth him on a pinnacle of the temple, And saith unto him, If thou be the Son of God, cast thyself down: for it is written, He shall give his angels charge concerning thee: and in their hands they shall bear thee up, lest at any time thou dash thy foot against a stone.*

*Jesus said unto him, It is written again, Thou shalt not tempt the Lord thy God.*

*Again, the devil taketh him up into an exceeding high mountain, and sheweth him all the kingdoms of the world, and the glory of them; And saith unto him, All these things will I give thee, if thou wilt fall down and worship me. Then saith Jesus unto him, Get thee hence, Satan: for it is written, Thou shalt worship the Lord thy God, and him only shalt thou serve. Then the devil leaveth him, and, behold, angels came and ministered unto him."*

This is a popular portion of the scriptures which talks about the temptation of our Lord Jesus Christ after His 40 days fasting and prayer in the wilderness. Although there are many lessons the Lord has taught and can still teach us from this experience of Jesus with Satan, there is this particular one He has put in my heart to share with you in this book.

If you take the time to carefully read from verses one to eleven, you will notice that the temptations were actually three (3) in number. The devil presented the first one to Jesus, but He responded by quoting the Word back to him; the second temptation followed the same trend and even the third.

However, if you pay attention to the response of Jesus to the devil upon presenting the third one, you will notice He said something He didn't say during the first and the second. Jesus said in verse 10 according to different translations *"...Be gone, Satan..."* (AMP, RSV), *"...Away with you, Satan..."* (NKJV), *"...Beat it, Satan..."* (MSG), *"...Away from me, Satan..."* (NIV), *"...Get out of here, Satan..."* (TLB, NLT), *"...Go away, Satan..."* (HCSB, GNT), *"...Get thee hence, Satan..."* (KJV, AKJV), *"...Go, Satan..."* (NASB), *"...Get behind me, Satan..."* (WEB), *"...Go away from me, Satan..."* (NCV).

And what did the devil do? He simply departed (went away from Him and stopped disturbing Him) just as Jesus demanded (verse 11).

But did you notice that the devil didn't leave until He was told to leave? That was what Eve did not do in the Garden of Eden. The moment Jesus said *"Get out of here, Satan"*, he simply got out and there was no 4th temptation. It ended right there.

James 4:7 says once you have submitted yourself to God, you are to resist (stop, prevent, hinder) the devil, (not discuss, negotiate, pray about or even cry about the devil). It is only then he will flee from you like he departed from Jesus. If you can live by this principle, I guarantee the devil will never mess around with you again.

If you feel any symptom of sickness or disease in your body, don't cry. Simply command like Jesus did, "Away from my body, Satan". If your child is misbehaving and all effort to help him has failed, simply resist the devil by saying "Get out of my child's life and affairs, Satan". Make sure you say it like Jesus did. Don't just say "get out", but "get out, Satan" so that he will know he's the one you are talking to.

But if you are not yet born again, it can't work. He will just laugh at you. Therefore, to live this way, YOU MUST BE BORN AGAIN. And this is the beauty of the whole thing; the moment you ask the devil to leave and he leaves, angels will come and minister to you, helping you to overcome the challenge at hand (Matthew 4:11). Hallelujah!

Say "Thank You Jesus for the revelation of Your Word".

Note: Keep meditating on these insights and prayerfully apply them to relevant areas of your life and even those of others. You are also free to share this with everyone you desire to see delivered from Satan's constant torture. You are victorious in Jesus' Name. Amen.

# Conclusion

So far, the Lord has revealed some biblical principles to us. The purpose is not just to know, document, or preach them, rather they were revealed so that we can walk in them.

According to John 8:32, only the truth that is known sets free. So, go through these principles one by one and determine to build your Christian walk around them for a life of Kingdom impact here on earth.

Jesus said in John 13:17(NLT) - *"You know these things- now do them! That is the path of blessing."*

May the Lord release upon you and your entire household the grace to walk worthy of His calling upon your lives in Jesus' Name!

# WHY YOU REALLY NEED JESUS!

You might have heard a lot of Preachers talk about the importance of surrendering one's life to Jesus and even the dangers of not doing so at one time or the other without you being really moved. But with these three (3) important reasons highlighted below, I strongly believe you will not need another sermon before deciding to yield to His saving grace regardless of your religious beliefs.

1. **You have an Enemy to overcome:** There is an adversary who is all out to steal from you, kill you and destroy you regardless of your level of education, moral uprightness, societal influence or even religious beliefs. He is Devil by name (John 10:10, 1 Peter 5: 8), and he doesn't release any of

his captives until he completely destroys their souls in hell. The ONLY One Who can deliver you from his manipulations and also save your soul from him is Jesus Christ.

2. **You have an Appointment to keep:** Being alive and reading this implies you have a very important and inevitable appointment to keep. It is an appointment with death (Hebrews 9:27). Death is the sure end of all mortals (of which you are part); and to enable you prepare for this appointment without fear of eternal damnation, you need Jesus. He is the ONLY One Who has power over death (Revelation 1:18).

3. **You have a Judge to face:** Upon departure from this earth, you will have to stand before a judgment throne to render an account of your earthly life (Hebrews 9:27, Romans 14:12). The outcome of this judgment is what will determine your eternal abode which will either be Heaven

or the Lake of fire. Interestingly, the Judge Who will preside over your case and also decide where you will spend your eternity is Jesus (John 5:21-30, 2 Timothy 4:1). I perceive you are thinking "is God not our Judge? Why Jesus?' Well, you are not wrong. But God the Father Himself is the One Who handed over all the judgment to His Son, Jesus Christ. Read the verse 22 of that John chapter 5. So Jesus is the ONLY One Who has the power to either judge you guilty or guiltless in eternity.

Now that you know these, the wisest thing you can do for yourself is to quickly establish a relationship with Jesus, since you don't even know how close your appointment with death is. To do this, say this prayer aloud:

*"Lord Jesus, I am a sinner and I cannot help myself. Wash me in your precious blood and make me a new creature. I open the door of my heart to you today, come into my life and become my Lord and Savior. Grant me the grace*

*to overcome the devil, prepare me for eternity and help me to escape the judgment reserved for sinners. Thank You Jesus for saving me. Amen."*

Congratulations! You are now SAVED. Go and sin no more.

To learn more about your new relationship with Jesus, kindly send an Email to info@gloem.org or emancipation4souls@yahoo.com, we will send you a material that will help you. You can also call, text, or send a WhatsApp message to +1 587 9735910 or +1 587 9695910 for further assistance.

And to learn more about God, His Word and His plans for your life, kindly visit our Facebook page [***https://www.facebook.com/gloem.org***] for daily meditation in the Word of God (all year round) and our Blog page [***https://gloem.org/myblog***] for life-transforming publications.

You are also invited to listen to Freedom Podcast: The Official Weekly Podcast of Global Emancipation Ministries – Calgary via https://anchor.fm/gloem

All these great resources capable of developing your spiritual stamina will help you become an overcomer in life regardless of what comes your way.

# PRAYER POINTS

1. Father, thank You for opening my eyes to the truths contained in this book.
2. Father, please cause every experience in my life to work together for my good.
3. I cancel everything contrary to my prosperity and advancement in Jesus' Name.
4. God of all possibilities, please cause my grass to become green again.
5. From today, the answers to my prayers shall no longer be delayed in Jesus' Name.
6. Father, beginning from now, please release upon me and my household the ability to walk with you and serve you faithfully in the Name of Jesus.
7. Father, I thank You for answering all my prayers. Glory be to Your Holy Name. Hallelujah!

# BECOME A FINANCIAL PARTNER WITH JESUS

At *Global Emancipation Ministries - Calgary*, our mandate is *to liberate men through the knowledge of the Truth* and our mission statement is *creating channels through which men can encounter the Truth - [Isaiah 61:1-3; John 8:32, 36; I Thessalonians 5:24]*.

**Our Ministerial Activities include** Rural and Urban Evangelical Outreaches, Prison Evangelism, Hospital Ministrations, Mobilization for Missions Support, Teaching of the undiluted Word of God, Scripture-Based Seminars, Discipleship, Training of Field Missionaries and Empowerment of underprivileged ones among other Field Ministerial Tasks.

If you sense the Lord is calling you to reach out to the lost by engaging in any of these activities or by assisting those involved with your resources, please feel free to join us. Let us come together as we take the Gospel of our Lord Jesus Christ to the hurting and forgotten ones. [Mark 16:15-20].

Please join us in these kingdom projects by making your weekly, monthly, quarterly, or annual donations to Global Emancipation Ministries – Calgary.

**You can visit the "GIVE" section on our website, www.gloem.org, to learn about the ways to give.**

For acknowledgment, please advise your donations to us by email: info@gloem.org or emancipation4souls@yahoo.com, and kindly include your details i.e. name, address, email, and location. Alternatively, you can simply call +1 587 9735910 to do same.

You can also volunteer your gifts and talents in the service of the Lord through our ministerial platforms regardless of your location. To get information on how to go about this, please visit www.gloem.org and contact us via email: info@gloem.org or emancipation4souls@yahoo.com.

God bless you.

# About the Author

By the special grace of God, **Anthony O. Adefarakan** is the privileged President of **Global Emancipation Ministries - Calgary (GLOEM)** with headquarters in Canada, North America, and **Emancipating Truth Ministry International (ETMI)** with headquarters in Nigeria, West Africa.

The Lord called him into the field ministry in February 2008 with the mandate to liberate men through the knowledge of the Truth, and by December 2012 he was ordained and commissioned as the Pioneer Pastor – in – Charge of The Redeemed Christian Church of God, Revelation Parish, Shalom Area under Delta Province III, Nigeria where he served until 1st February 2015 when he officially handed over to a new Pastor in order to focus on his field ministry to which the Lord had earlier called him and for which the authority of the church had already prayed and released him to undertake.

On 29th September 2013, he was awarded a Post Graduate Diploma in Tent – Making Mission from the Redeemed Christian School of Missions, Nigeria (RECSOM, Asaba Campus) where he also had the privilege to train Pastors and Missionaries as a lecturer in 2017.

Since the commissioning of his field ministry in 2015 he has had the opportunity to lead his ministry officers to field ministrations in different Prisons, Hospitals, Orphanages, Rural communities, Camp settlements, Markets, Local churches among other places with great successes on all occasions – such as the salvation of sinners, healing of the sick, financial empowerment of mission churches, provision of relief materials to the poor, provision of medical services to the underprivileged, baptism in the Holy Ghost, deliverance from demonic oppression, the release of inmates just to mention a few - all to the glory of God Who alone is the Doer.

He is the author of other best-selling titles such as *The Law of Kinds, Learning From the Ants, The Immutability of God's Counsel, Surely there is an End, Life Applicable lessons from the Book of Ruth, One thing is Needful Weekly Devotional Guide, Life Applicable Revelations from God's Word* (Volumes 1 and 2) among others.

He is blissfully married to Ifeoluwa A. Adefarakan and their marriage is fruitful to the glory of God.

**Jesus is his Message, Freedom is the Outcome! Isaiah 61:1-3**

www.ingramcontent.com/pod-product-compliance
Lightning Source LLC
Chambersburg PA
CBHW021431070526
44577CB00001B/154